SERMONS

Application of Legal Principles and Procedures in the Life and Ministry of Christ

CHARLES MWEWA

ACP
2023

Republished by:

AFRICA IN CANADA PRESS (ACP)

Ottawa, Ontario,

Canada

www.acpress.ca

www.charlesmwewa.com

ISBN: 978-1-988251-30-1

DEDICATION

To an unknown person who left a pile of legal
materials that arrested my interest in the law –
whoever you were or wherever you are, this book is
yours.

CONTENTS

PREFACE

Ethics or moral judgment is at the center of biblical interpretation. Jesus Christ is said to be the lawyer of lawyers, in the sense that, no-one had ever propounded the legal efficacy and representation of Scripture more than Him – and no-one has, ever since. In His sayings can be found the saliences of the English Law, from equity, to common-law, to statutory jurisprudence. Jesus Christ is the quintessential jurist.

In these sermons, I expostulate on both the legal efficacy and representation central to the Gospels, in particular, and the Bible, in general. Written from a rare legal dynamic, these sermons evoke a sense of responsibility for those who are impacted by its truths. The content can be used by ordained Ministers, the lay people, and for reference. The authority comes from the Scripture, highlighted throughout the book in footnotes. Those who seek judicial justice and those who cleave for spiritual ascendancy, are united in the topics selected for this purpose. This book, therefore, is for both legal minds and those who love God's justice in the affairs of men and nations.

c.m.

1 | AN INIQUITOUS TRIAL

"Who has believed our message? And to whom has the arm of the LORD been revealed? He grew up before Him like a tender shoot, and like a root out of dry ground. He had no stately form or majesty to attract us, no beauty that we should desire Him. He was despised and rejected by men, a man of sorrows, acquainted with grief. Like one from whom men hide their faces, He was despised, and we esteemed Him not. Surely, He took on our infirmities and carried our sorrows; yet we considered Him stricken by God, struck down and afflicted. But He was pierced for our transgressions, He was crushed for our iniquities; the punishment that brought us peace was upon Him, and by His stripes we are healed," (Isaiah 53:1-4).

Introduction

In the case of *R. v. Sussex Justices*, a 1924 case, Lord Hewart, the then Lord Chief Justice of England, had laid down a dictum of, "Justice must not only be done but must also be seen to be done." Rome, and England, were some of the earliest places were law and justice developed.

A Byzantine Emperor, Justinian's Code of Justinian (Latin: *Codex Justinianus*) had long permeated Europe in the seventh century before the Viking hero, William the Conqueror, had conquered England in 1066 and thereafter introduced the Common-Law.

At His trial, it was neither by Roman law, nor by Mosaic canon, that our Lord was condemned and killed. It was by political intrigue and conspired malice. In this sermon, it is argued that the Roman and Jewish rulers conspired to deny our Lord justice. And to assist in the investigation of this theme, the following points will be used: Arrest through betrayal; witnesses in denial; and injustice in expedited trial. The points will be discussed in that order before a conclusion, application and related prayer are offered.

1. Arrest through Betrayal

The Byzantines, who were superior and the masters in laws, believed that betrayal was one of the worst sins. Traitors faced very unorthodoxy deaths. And there was no worse traitor than the one with whom you shared either a table or a bed. Our Lord, Jesus Christ, hand-picked His disciples who sat and ate at His table, and yet one of them betrayed Him: "'When evening came, Jesus was reclining with the twelve disciples. And while they were eating, He said to them, 'Truly I tell you, one of you will betray Me.... Jesus answered, 'The one who has dipped his hand into the bowl with Me will betray Me.'"[1]

Judas Iscariot sat and shared a meal with Jesus. He also kept the group's money. He betrayed his Lord. In His time, thus, our Lord received the worst betrayal ever. If He were married, the worst betrayal would come from a spouse. In this case, it came from the most trusted disciple. It is no wonder after Judas realized what he had done, committed suicide.[2] Traitors were understood to have been dupes of Satan himself. Thus, "Then entered Satan into Judas surnamed Iscariot, being of the number of the twelve."[3] This is consistent with what the

---

[1] Matthew 26:21 and 23
[2] See Matthew 27:1–10
[3] Luke 22:3-23

ancient perceived betrayal to be; it was an act of evil, sanctioned by the devil himself.

Our Lord knew that Satan was involved in His arrest. He never resisted: "Jesus, knowing all that was going to happen to him, went out and asked them, 'Who is it you want?' 'Jesus of Nazareth,' they replied. 'I am he,' Jesus said. (And Judas the traitor was standing there with them.) When Jesus said, 'I am he,' they drew back and fell to the ground."[4]

Note that Jesus presented Himself to be arrested. He allowed it. In judicial parlance, the innocent do not get arrested, only the alleged guilty. Similarly, those who are to be arrested usually fight or flee. Our Lord surrendered Himself as though He was guilty; He was not. He even healed Malchus whom Peter had chopped his ear off.[5] Satan brought two factions which hated each other together in order to arrest Jesus: "The detachment of soldiers with its commander and the Jewish officials arrested Jesus."[6] Betrayers usually connive with enemies and evildoers to inflict injustices on the innocent or the loved ones. That is why betrayal is such an awful act.

---

[4] John 18: 4-6
[5] See Matthew 26:51; Mark 14:47; Luke 22:5
[6] John 18:12

2. Witnesses in Denial

Do you know what a lawyer's worst nightmare is? It is when her material witness either refuses to testify or he does testify but changes sides. It does not matter the amount of preparation; the circus is tangled. In the art of presentation of evidence, the rules require an advocate at this time to treat her own witness as hostile and cross examine him.

In the case of our Lord, the most powerful witness – who ate with the Lord, saw miracles firsthand and even experienced one himself, and who was shaping up to be the leader, cowered and denied his Lord: "Simon Peter and another disciple were following Jesus. Because this disciple was known to the high priest, he went with Jesus into the high priest's courtyard, but Peter had to wait outside at the door. The other disciple, who was known to the high priest, came back, spoke to the servant girl on duty there and brought Peter in. 'You aren't one of this man's disciples too, are you?' she asked Peter. He replied, 'I am not.'"[7]

Do you know why this is surprising? Peter was not being asked by a lawyer or a soldier; it was an innocuous servant, and a girl. In those days, girl servants had the lowest social status. In other words, there was no threat to Peter. He simply denied His Lord. If Peter couldn't testify

---

[7] *Ibid.*, verves 15- 17

for Jesus, who would? With no witnesses, His defence would have fallen on deaf-eared judges. Of course, the outcome would have been conviction and sentencing. In this case, death.

The Lord warned: "Many will say to Me on that day, 'Lord, Lord, did we not prophesy in Your name, and in Your name drive out demons and perform many miracles?' Then I will tell them plainly, 'I never knew you; depart from Me, you workers of lawlessness!'"[8] You see the power of a witness.

When we stand before God, we will have only Jesus to testify in our defence. If we did not accept Him and did what He wanted, we would be left with no witness. Thanks be to God, those whom the Father has given to Christ will not be condemned: "All that the Father gives Me will come to Me, and the one who comes to Me I will certainly not cast out."[9]

In other words, Christ will be their witness. Now, you understand one of the reasons why the Lord's trial was iniquitous. His trusted man betrayed Him, and His most present disciple denied testifying for Him.

---

[8] Matthew 7:22-23
[9] John 6:37

3. Injustice in Expedited Trial

The fundamental reason why trials are held is to find the truth. In this trial, truth became *anathema*: "'If I said something wrong,' Jesus replied, 'testify as to what is wrong. But if I spoke the truth, why did you strike me?'"[10] The Jewish leaders failed to find even a single lie in Jesus using their own Mosaic Law.

The High Priest tried the entire night but in vain. Seeing that the Mosaic Law gave them no breakthrough, they sent Him to a Roman Governor: "Then the Jewish leaders took Jesus from Caiaphas to the palace of the Roman governor. By now it was early morning, and to avoid ceremonial uncleanness they did not enter the palace, because they wanted to be able to eat the Passover. So, Pilate came out to them and asked, 'What charges are you bringing against this man? 'If he were not a criminal,' they replied, 'we would not have handed him over to you.' Pilate said, 'Take him yourselves and judge him by your own law.' 'But we have no right to execute anyone,' they objected."[11]

The above, is inimical even in banana republics. First, they find Him innocent using Judaism's law. What do they do, you would think they would release Him, oh, no. They send Him to a totally wrong jurisdiction. Rome did not meddle

---

[10] John 18:23
[11] *Ibid.*, verses 28-31

into the local and customary Jewish jurisprudential affairs. Second, they had no charges against Him to warrant change of jurisdiction. "Criminality" is not a charge; it is a condition that only obtains after one has been properly and legally convicted. But the Jewish leaders had already condemned Jesus even before the trial began. In fact, they had already passed sentence ("we have no right to execute anyone," they said. Implying that Jesus deserved execution). They had already decided on the sentence even before the trial was over. And last, they changed suddenly from a Jewish law accusation to Roman insurrection accusation, just to force the Roman gubernatorial to claim jurisdiction.

Then came the worst of the worst. "'What is truth?' retorted Pilate. With this he went out again to the Jews gathered there and said, 'I find no basis for a charge against him.'"[12] Law had failed. There was no basis in law to either charge Jesus or convict Him. In normal situations, this should have ended everything. The accused must have been released. But no, the Jews, who, hitherto, had no love relationship with their colonial emperor, now, suddenly, became political and threatened Pilate. You see, in Roman political system, Caesar was law. If one went against Caesar, they danced with death. Pilate was an appointee of Caesar, and the Jews knew exactly how to blow the whistle: "From

---

[12] *Ibid.*, verse 38

then on, Pilate tried to set Jesus free, but the Jewish leaders kept shouting, 'If you let this man go, you are no friend of Caesar. Anyone who claims to be a king opposes Caesar.'[13]

What did they do, they blackmailed Pilate. He would do nothing, though He tried to be fair and suggested a choice for the Jews between Barabbas (an insurrectionist) and Jesus (a holy man). You guessed right, they chose an insurrectionist and demanded to kill Jesus.

Thus, the Jewish leaders used every trick in the book of evil and injustice to rush Jesus through an iniquitous trial and condemn Him to death. Isaiah says that all this was predicted to happen for the salvation of many: "Who has believed our message? And to whom has the arm of the LORD been revealed?" Indeed, if this report had not been substantiated by historical reality, who would have thought that those entrusted with law and justice would have been the same to conspire with evil and condemn a just person.

Conclusion & Application

You see, justice must not only be done, but it must also be seen to be done. In our Lord's trial, justice was nowhere nearby. It had gone. His own confidante betrayed Him, his most reliable

---

[13] John 19:12

witness denied Him, and those entrusted with the management of the law, abused it against Him. We must be careful that we don't connive with evil to betray those who love us and are entrusted to us. We should be careful that we don't let down our loved ones and brethren just when our testimony is required to support them. And we should not use the instruments of mercy and truth to deal evilly with people around us. Law must be an instrument of justice, and a mechanism for finding truth, and not for hurting truth. Each time we betray our loved ones, we become dupes of Satan.

Related Prayer

Lord, mercy and truth, grant, we pray, in abundance;
In times of weakness, guard our faith with substance;
When faced with betrayal, recuse us from Satan's hell;
And if we should forget justice, let also our joy fail.

In Jesus' name, our Lord,
    Amen.

2 | THE LAW OF HAPPINESS

*"But godliness with contentment is great gain.
For we brought nothing into the world, and we
can take nothing out of it. But if we have food
and clothing, we will be content with that,"* (1
Timothy 6:6-12).

Introduction

In English law, under the auspices of equity,
there is a rule against unjust enrichment. It
happens when a person makes themselves
rich at the expense of another's misfortune. The
Courts, usually, impose an obligation that the
subject of unjust enrichment repays (or
restitutes) the victim of the said unjust
enrichment. Similarly, in Roman law, there is a
similar maxim: *Nemo locupletari potest aliena iactura
or nemo locupletari debet cum aliena iactura* or "no-

one should be benefited at another's expense." The Bible gives a warning to those who are discontented in life. In this sermon, three points are discussed to elucidate on the law of happiness, namely: Godliness with contentment is great gain; we brought nothing into the world; and we can take nothing out of the world. The points will be discussed in that order before a conclusive application and a prayer are given.

1. Godliness with Contentment is Great Gain

At the heart of human happiness, is the idea that one is contented with who they are, what they have and where they live. The anchoring for more and desire to have more, is, perhaps, the greatest avarice against happiness. The other day, this author was observing animals and birds. They were born with only one set of apparel. They do not change clothes and yet they seem contented.

Flowers, however pretty, are born and do die with their original color. Only human beings (and to some extent snakes and chameleons) are born with the ability to change clothes and appearances. However, animals and birds are contented. God has placed within them the ability to self-renewal. In principle, every human being is capable of survival with only one pair of clothes. But experience shows that people are discontented when they have fewer clothes. Some purchase things they do not even need.

Consider food, for example. It does not matter what kind of food one eats; what matters is that they get filled and gain energy to live by. However, we see people going for wantonness and gluttony – buying food for play and pleasure. Meanwhile, the rich and wealthy do throw away food while the poor and needy are dying with hunger.

And it is the same with accommodation and housing. All a person needs is a place comfortable enough for them to be warm and safe. However, we see people anchoring for mansions (and sometimes they have more empty rooms than they can fill). Meanwhile, there are homeless people and the poor with large families who can only manage a single room.

The rule is, no-one gets happy because they have more clothes, more food or more space. For "the earth is the LORD's, and everything in it."[14] The Lord God owns everything seen and unseen. And He said, "Therefore do not worry about tomorrow...."[15]

---

[14] 1 Corinthians 10:26
[15] Matthew 6:34

Now imagine how gracious God has been. He makes His sun to rise for all – and no matter where you live, there are rivers, grasses, soil, and clean air. He has given to all liberally. Even birds with very little intellectual prowess, do not go hungry or unrenewed: "Look at the birds of the air; they do not sow or reap or store away in barns, and yet your Heavenly Father feeds them. Are you not much more valuable than they?"[16]

Happiness is knowing who you are in God – the understanding that God has not only provided for everything, but also that, by faith, no matter where you live, God will always supply your daily bread. All you need to do is pray, "And it shall be given to you."[17]

But also remember that for food, clothes and covering, God will always provide for you, either via nature or the agency of humans. And the good example is in the next point.

2. We Brought Nothing into the World

The author is a proud father of three daughters. Each time one was born, he was present. And there is no better place than the delivery room where this realization hits home. Babies, indeed,

---

[16] Matthew 6:26
[17] Luke 11:9

are born with nothing – no clothes, no food, and no shelter.

What is amazing is the fact that, instinctively, birds, animals and humans prepare for the new-borns. But it is not, in fact, parents doing the preparations. God provides the capacity to care for the young ones – and this is common among all living things. God cares for the young ones through the adults. He never abandons any.

Within a minute or less of its birth, a child will receive clothes, milk, and shelter. How did all that happen? Because its creator pre-positioned everything. It was not me or you who got ready; God moved the parents to prepare for the young ones.

Now reason with yourself, if God cared for the innocuous and hopeless baby until the time it could fend for itself, how will He abandon you later? God does not change,[18] and, therefore, none of His creation will perish due to hunger, thirst, or lack of shelter.

What then causes lack or poverty, you may ask? It is chiefly due to people's selfishness and greed. God has provided sufficient natural resources for all peoples everywhere. But some, due to selfishness and greed, have amassed more than they can possibly utilize.

---

[18] Malachi 3:6

There are many selfish people in our world who have more than an entire nation can own, and yet some people in the same world are dying from hunger, thirst, and lack of covering. Even if those with such large amounts of wealth were to live one hundred more years, they would not exhaust all that they have accumulated. But due to selfishness and greed, they would not as take a small portion and share it with the needy.

They will die unhappy, and so will the needy. Had they shared, they would have lived and died happy, and so would have those they shared with. It is just that simple. And the true reality comes, to all, at the time of death – because at this juncture, all, without exception, come to terms with the reality that they would not be taking anything with them, and this leads this author to the last point.

3. We Can Take Nothing Out of the World

This author-preacher was driving along a cemetery one day. And a thought hit him sharply: "All those graves there, with nothing but dead bones – some of those lying there were wealthy and influential, but death had brought them to the same level with those who had little on earth."

Now think about it, tomorrow you may die, and this thinker promises you that you will be lucky to die with an undergarment on you – probably thanks to the kindness of those who are still living.

But if all of us should die by nuclear means, it would mean all of us would perish with nothing. Indeed, we can take nothing out of the world. This, by itself is a revelation – that since we cannot take anything from this world, we are, then just custodians of God's creation. We are born, are given a portion to manage and when we die, we leave it for another to tend. And this is all there is to life. As the Apostle Paul has educated, "This, then, is how you ought to regard us: as servants of Christ and as those entrusted with the mysteries God has revealed."[19] And again, "Yes, each of us will give a personal account to God."[20]

So, then, we should be wise, and remember always to be who we are, custodians of God's creation. The sad truth is that we do not control our exist from the earth, just as we did not control our entry. That should be enough to teach us wisdom: "But God said to him, 'You fool! This very night your life will be demanded from you. Then who will get what you have prepared for yourself?"[21]

In his brief lamentations, Solomon mourns, "I hated all for which I had toiled under the sun,

---

[19] 1 Corinthians 4:1
[20] Romans 14:12
[21] Luke 12:20

because I must leave it to the man who comes after me. And who knows whether that man will be wise or foolish? Yet he will take over all the labor at which I have worked skillfully under the sun. This too is futile."[22]

True wisdom is investing in Heaven. And how does one invest in Heaven? There are three ways:

First, give to the poor and the needy – these will appreciate you greatly and say a prayer for you – with thanksgiving. If possible, do not only give to those who will favor you in return. Rather, give to those whose favor will come from their deep-faithed prayers.

Second, be contented. If you have more than you need, it means you have become a conduit for God to bless another – "It is more blessed to give than to receive."[23] Do not be like those selfish thieves who use this verse for their own enrichment. They tell you that it is more blessed to give than to receive because they are coveting your wealth, money, and resources, but they themselves never give even a penny to those in need.

---

[22] Ecclesiastes 2:18-19
[23] Acts 20:35

And third, know that you are a guardian/custodian of God's interests – do not forget this principle. If you should pray, work hard, or inherit great wealth – it is because God has His creation in mind. You are God's hands here on earth (God's partners tending to His creation on earth), God's willing supplier of His graces to others.

This balance is what makes, not only individuals, but even nations happier. The UN World Happiness Report conveniently named the Scandinavian countries as the happiest in the world, and the reason given is that of increased social support.

Happiness is partly a spiritual and partly a social construct. No-one is truly happy if they are ungodly, and the same is true, they are not happy if the neighbor is not. Pride, jealousies, and competitions in this context are not sanctioned by God – they are devilish mechanism for ramping up unhappiness in the world.

Where people truly share in truth, they will be happy, and this includes governments that make available legislations that promote food, clothing, and accommodation sufficiency.

How blessed the Lord's words: "The poor you will always have with you,"[24] so that, in part, we may always experience the happiness of giving and living for others.

Conclusion & Application

Stated simply, the Law of Happiness reads, living for spiritual and material contentment and the joy of meeting the needs of God's creatures. In cultures where they emphasize receiving, the majority of the people usually struggle to make ends meet. To be happy, truly happy, you will learn to live within your means – appreciating that all that you are and have come from God. All we have is short-lived, it remains behind when we die.

Wisdom demands that we take good care of all the blessings God has bestowed upon us. Everyone on earth is blessed – if they have clothes on them, have meals and can find a place where to sleep. The quality of one's clothes, food or shelter does not negate this fact. Greed and selfishness parade themselves as fashionistas – provoking and tempting people to despise God's blessings upon them, because, in comparison to others, they deem their own blessings of inferior nature and quality.

---

[24] Matthew 26:11

Everything God has made is of quality; it is humans who label things more superior to others. If what you have makes you warm, filled and comfortable, you are blessed.[25] Having fifty sets of clothes or seven vehicles or an eighteen-roomed house does not make one happy just as one only needs one attire at a time, one room at a time and one meal at a time. God will, and has, already provided all that we need for godliness and health.

And last, remember the words of the preacher: "What has been will be again, what has been done will be done again; there is nothing new under the sun," (Ecclesiastes 1:9). So, do not enrich yourself at the expense of others, and be happy by being contented.

---

[25] Read Charles Mwewa, *Ten Financial & Wealth Attitudes to Avoid* (Ottawa: ACP, 2021), for a comprehensive review of the right attitudes to have towards money and wealth.

Related Prayer

Dear Heavenly Father,

Give us a spirit of gratitude, so that we may
appreciate what we already have;
Give us a peace that surpasses all
understanding, that comes from above;
Give us humility, so we can remain true in
whatever state we may be found;
Give us contentment, so that pride, greed, and
selfishness we may confound;

In Jesus' name, our Lord,
Amen!

3 | GRACE – GOD'S STANDARD OF PROOF

"My grace is sufficient for you…" (2
Corinthians 12:9a);

*"For it is by grace you have been saved through
faith, and this not from yourselves; it is the gift of
God, not by works, so that no one can boast,"*
(Ephesians 2:8-9).

Introduction

One of the ways in which the law serves justice, is that it prescribes standards by which allegations must be proven. In democratic societies, both defendants and the accused are given an opportunity to provide a defence or to defend themselves. This process is variedly called due-process, rule of natural justice or the right to be heard, or procedural fairness, or even the rule of law.

The legal standards to prove matters are based on a scale of balance – serious offences are allocated very high thresholds, while less serious offences have very low standards. Generally, there are four common standards: For crimes, it is beyond a reasonable doubt; for civil wrongs, it is on the balance of probabilities; for administrative infractions, it is based on reasonable apprehension of bias; and for immigration/refugee cases, it is usually the "clear and convincing" standard.

Offences attract more or less rigorous standards depending on the constitutive structure of the offence. Thus, crimes have a more rigorous standard than civil wrongs or regulatory and administrative offences.

In this sermon, we contrast the legal standard of a crime to the New Testament divine standard of grace and ascertain that God's grace is amazingly an uncommon blessing. The following points will be discussed: The criminal standard; the sin standard; and the grace standard. The points will be delivered in that order before rendering a conclusion with its related prayer.

1. The Criminal Standard

In criminal law, to convict an accused defendant, the Crown (the State or the Director of Public Prosecutions or the People) must prove a case beyond a reasonable doubt. That is, they must establish that the accused both thought evil of doing a crime (or *mens rea*) and that they, in fact, put those thoughts in action and acted evilly (or *actus reas*).

The establishing of these two elements is a very rigorous and highly standardized process. Both elements must be present to be convicted. Otherwise, if only one is present, the accused will be acquitted. Thus, you can think of killing someone but as long as you do not follow-up on those "evil thoughts" with attendant actions, a crime is not committed. And *vice versa*, if you kill someone without a requisite *mens rea* present, such as killing someone while asleep or while being temporarily insane or without mental capacity or while being a minor child, a crime is equally not committed. The Crown must prove that both elements are present for the Court to convict.

2. The Sin Standard

There is only one element to sin, it is akin to a legal principle of absolute liability or a single-element culpability regime. One act or a single thought is enough to warrant guiltiness. Thus, "But I tell you that anyone who looks at a woman lustfully has already committed adultery with her in his heart."[26] This is the only requirement to sin, either think it or do it.

The only defence one has is either don't think it or don't do it. Before grace, it was nearly impossible to avoid sin culpability. In the Old Testament, the standard was known as the "Glorious Standard," and none, if anything, was able to reach it. It was unattainable. Therefore, it is truthful to state, "For everyone has sinned; we all fall short of God's glorious standard."[27]

If one was appearing before the Judgment Seat of God, before the grace dispensation, they had neither a lawyer nor a mediator. They had a notoriously very high standard (Glorious Standard) to prove their innocence. They were to prove sinlessness by stating categorically that they either did not do the alleged sin or they did not think it.

---

26 Matthew 5:28
27 Romans 3:23 (New Living Translation)

If they thought it, did it or both, they were culpable. The penalty for sin is, and was, death: "For the wages of sin is death…"[28] There was no room for error, no excuses, and no salvation from sin.

The old regime would only allow for temporary pacification of God's wrath through equally very rigorous sacrificial offerings through the blood of innocent animals. All this did, was to cover sin, albeit temporarily, so that God would not be revulsed by it. It neither forgave sin nor cleaned it. So, God was still searching for a more perfect system – that would both forgive and clean sin and would provide for an effective clemency procedure – such as with effective lawyering before His throne. But thanks be to God, because these were accomplished through one Person, Jesus Christ.[29]

First, Christ became the sacrifice itself – perfect and blameless: "For by one sacrifice he has made perfect forever those who are being made holy."[30] Note here that perfection precedes holiness. At the point of salvation, we are made perfect before God. However, the process of becoming holy (or sanctification) goes on throughout our matriculation period till we die.

---

[28] Romans 6:23

[29] For a comprehensive study on law and grace, read, Charles Mwewa, *Law & Grace* (Ottawa, ACP, 2021).

[30] Hebrews 10:14

The reason we are perfect at salvation is because God now relates to us through the Person of His Son: "God made him who had no sin to be sin for us, so that in him we might become the righteousness of God."[31] Note that Christ did not become a "sinner," rather, He became sin itself.

God was dealing with the problem of sin once and for all. God, literally, placed all of the world's sin on His Son, and by that act, once and forever, He punished sin. And in the same act, He permanently liberated from sin those who had lived under its bondage.

Second, Christ became the witness to the substance and process of redemption. Historically, lasting covenants were sealed with blood. One own's blood served as an undisputable witness to a permanent covenant. Christ was the witness to the New Covenant by His own blood: "This is my blood of the covenant, which is poured out for many for the forgiveness of sins."[32]

The insufficiency of the Old Covenant was in this respect: The blood used was from animals, so, it was temporary. The animals had to die, so, they were left with no witness. However, the New Covenant is permanent because of its sufficiency: It was made through the spotless

---

[31] 2 Corinthians 5:21
[32] Matthew 26:28

blood of Christ. The one who gave the blood is a permanent witness because He rose again to testify to the covenant. The Lamb (Christ) is first present in Heaven: "Then I saw a Lamb, looking as if it had been slain, standing at the center of the throne, encircled by the four living creatures and the elders,"[33] and second, He lawyers for us: "Who then will condemn us? No one—for Christ Jesus died for us and was raised to life for us, and he is sitting in the place of honor at God's right hand, *pleading for us*."[34]

Note how intricately this verse announces all the sufficiency of the New Covenant: Condemnation of sin is dealt with. The sacrifice died and resurrected. The witness is present in Heaven. And Christ is now a lawyer pleading for us. And the next point, we will answer to the question: By what standard does Christ lawyers for us now?

3. The Grace Standard

When you sin, you have an advocate before God to plead your case: "My dear children, I write this to you so that you will not sin. But if anybody does sin, we have an advocate with the Father – Jesus Christ, the Righteous One."[35] Each time you come before God, Christ

---

[33] Revelation 5:6
[34] Romans 8:34 (emphasis added)
[35] 1 John 2:1

presents a motion for acquittal (which has already been completed through Him). He appears on your behalf both as witness and advocate (pleader or lawyer). And the standard of proof is Grace – it is not based on whether you think the sin or you act it out – with Grace, you are announced free, guiltless, and forgiven just for doing nothing but putting your faith in Christ's work.

In other words, if you trust Jesus with your case, the win is guaranteed. It is by Grace (standard of proof) that you have been saved (freed, acquitted, forgiven, let go, made whole again, and etc.) through faith (by simply trusting in the competent work of your lawyer, Jesus Christ).

Call it a mystery or God's unmerited favor to us, or simply amazing – by Grace we can have guaranteed confidence that no matter what we have done or said, we will receive absolution in God's presence: "Let us then approach God's throne of grace with confidence, so that we may receive mercy and find grace to help us in our time of need."[36] This verse is a crown jewelry of divine order, for the following three reasons:

First, God's throne has changed from one of judgment to one of Grace. We do not come before God to be judged, but to be vindicated or justified. Second, no matter what we have done or said, we receive mercy from God.

---

[36] Hebrews 4:16

Remember, "Mercy triumphs over judgment."[37] But we must ask for mercy (you cannot receive what you have not asked for). Third, the sufficiency of Grace – that we may find it in our time of need. In another place God has announced, thus, "My grace is sufficient for you."[38] All these are found only where God the Father and the Son are – in God's presence.

Conclusion & Application

Grace, is the lowest standard ever known in the history of creation. Grace needs no proof. Grace demands no evidence. Grace is free for and to all – and all it takes is only to put one's trust (faith) in Christ Jesus. There is no sin that does not bow before the blazing flurries of Grace. There is no sin too high or too low that the Standard of Grace cannot bring to balance. Even sins that are done or said deliberately are not beyond the reach of Grace.

And the reason is because Grace is a double-edged sword – it is a standard and it is also a teacher" "For the grace of God has appeared, bringing salvation to everyone. It instructs us to renounce ungodliness and worldly passions, and to live sensible, upright, and godly lives in the present age."[39]

---

[37] James 2:13
[38] 2 Corinthians 12:9a
[39] Titus 2:11-12

If human institutions have condemned you, it is because their standards of proof are too high. But with God, your chances of forgiveness are one hundred percent. There is absolutely no condemnation to those who put their trust in Christ. And because the spiritual standard of proof is low or non-existent, it is possible that most people will make it to Heaven even with a simple confession at their death beds. It is possible to be pure, even when you are constantly making mistakes. It is that mysterious – it is called Grace.

Related Prayer

Dear Heavenly Father,

It cannot be said with words what You have
done for mankind through Christ;
His death, is now our perfect life, and in His
blood, a perfect Lamb you've sacrificed;
I pray, that men and women and children
everywhere, would in You put their trust;
And when they sin, forgive, and no matter
how dark their deeds, declare them just.

In Jesus' name, our Lord,
Amen.

4 | THE REALITY OF FAITH

"Now faith is the substance of things hoped for, the evidence of things not seen," (Hebrews 11:1, KJV).

Introduction

In this sermon, we will consider the topic of Faith. We will provide a thematic review of the "Reality of Faith." Faith, is more real than both reason and reality. And the assumption is that what we sense is less real than what we can only perceive with the mind of Faith. To assist us to make a thorough review of this subject, we will discuss the following three points: Faith is the substance; Faith is the evidence; and Faith is the confidence. We will proceed with this sermon in that order before we make a conclusive application of the principles we will learn. We will end with a related prayer.

1. Faith is the Substance

The author of the book to the Hebrews defines Faith as, "…the substance of things hoped for…" in Hebrews 11:1.[40] Faith is not illusion, a far-fetched or distant reality; Faith is the present reality perceived by the senses of the unseen reality.

For anything to be a substance, it should, of necessity, not be spiritual, a fiction of imagination or an unreachable reality. A substance is a material reality, a thing. In essence, it is something you can see, feel, touch, smell, hear, and taste. In short, it is anything capable of being perceived and identified by the human sensory mechanism.

A substance exists in the realm of human mental and sensory circumference. It can be sensualized. A substance is a thing, and, therefore, it can be experienced. Between the womb and the tomb exists this dome we call reality. It enables us to be human and experience things as we view them now. It excludes non-matter and, in this real, physical realm, if you can't see anything, can't feel it, can't touch it, can't smell it, can't hear it, or can't taste it – then, it doesn't exist.

---

[40] King James Version or KJV

However, Faith connects us to the reality that we can't see and materializes the "things" that exist beyond the realm of reality. Thus, "...faith is the *reality* of what is hoped for, the proof of what is not seen."[41] Emphasis here is on, "reality."

2. Faith is the Evidence

In law, evidence is that which proves material facts. Evidence is proof. There is no legal proceeding that succeeds without evidence, even if such a process may be based in equity.[42] The Courts will award remedies to a party that has evidence, or where the absence of evidence is served by two exceptions, that of judicial notice or of a legal presumption. The standard of proof may be one of overwhelming evidence, such us beyond a reasonable doubt as it is in criminal matters. Or, it could be one of preponderance or predominance, in situations of civil litigation on a 51-49 percentage basis, commonly referred to as on the balance of probabilities.

---

[41] Hebrews 11:1, CSB (emphasis added)

[42] A body of English law which was developed in the Court of Chancery. It provides legal solutions or resolutions known as remedies where neither law nor precedence is able to. In other words, it proves a case simply based on what is fair or equitable.

Faith is said to be "the evidence of things not seen"[43] or the "the proof of what is not seen."[44] This notion cannot be fathomed within the scope of our "normal" sensory stipulations. It requires extra-sensory cogitation. In other words, it goes beyond the realm of our everyday thinking and perception.

In reality, you can't have evidence for that which is not seen. The "unseen nature" is the prerequisite for the absence of evidence. If you appeared before a Judge and claimed that you had evidence, but the Courts could not see it, you would be considered to be either insane or a clown. You will lose your case, no matter how simple the course of action. To be evidence, something must be seen. To be proof, it must be perceived by physical senses.

Faith is the evidence of what is not seen by the physical optical sensory system. It is perceived by spiritual "senses." To the person schooled in extrasensory perception (faith),[45] to a person who "believes," the unseen is as real as the seen. And it is imperative that humans pay attention to this aspect. To a child, as long as she can't see

---

[43] Hebrews 11:1, KJV

[44] *Ibid*, CSB

[45] Faith may also be defined as extrasensory perception, and this is not the same as ESP commonly adjudged in mystic and paranormal observatories. Such has no basis in the Bible and is used strictly for psychic or telepathic mysticism. The train of thought in both is similar; the difference lies in motivation. In Faith, the motive is the glorification of God, and not man or the devil.

water but only an ice block, she thinks, erroneously, that there is no water. However, to a mature person, water is present, albeit in a solid form of matter. An adult understands that water may exist in three forms of matter: Gas, liquid or solid. So, in whatever form water may exist, to an adult, water is still present.

Once you believe that you have something, having seen it with the eyes of Faith, you have presented God with evidence of what you need or desire. Thus, "If you believe, you will receive whatever you ask for in prayer."[46] Not everyone who prays may receive. There is a condition to it. They must first believe, and then what is immaterial in nature will be transformed into a material reality.

It is a spiritual principle. In vernacular, Faith is the heat that melts solid into liquid and evaporates liquids into gases, and the chemical reactivity that crystalizes gases into solids. Without this knowledge, you may die of thirst, when water had always existed around you.

Faith is not only the evidence a supplicant takes before God, but it is also the instrument God, the Great Judge, uses to award rewards (answered prayers). For Faith is also defined as "...the *conviction* of things not seen."[47] Faith is the final verdict or sentence that the unseen, in

---

[46] Matthew 21:22
[47] Hebrews 11:1, ESV (emphasis added)

fact, exists. And once that conviction is certified, it cements that fact that the things desired are here and now and can presently be utilized into manifest reality. Thus, healing will manifest, breakthroughs will manifest, salvation will manifest, finances or jobs or opportunities will all manifest, and so on. For everyone who believes, receives.[48]

3. Faith is the Confidence

The word "confidence" is translated Faith. It is the assurance that the things you hope for, will be yours. It is notable throughout the Bible that hope precedes Faith. One may have hope without Faith; however, no-one can have Faith without hope.

Hope is necessary to Faith. It is important to bear this in mind: Hope includes wishes, aspirations, desires, beliefs, optimism, chances, expectation, ambition, aim, plan, yearning, longing, dreams, hankering, craving and promises.

---

[48] See Acts 10:43, Mark 16:16, John 3:36, Romans 10:9-14, John 11:25-26,
Matthew 21:22, Hebrews 6:15, Hebrews 10: 19,22.

Hope feels, desires, and expects that certain things will happen. It is that strong expectation, that desire, that dream, that confidence that makes Faith show up. It costs nothing. You lose nothing. You gain everything.

Conclusion & Application

As sermonized, Faith is more real than reason or what is called "reality." What we already see were the works of original Faith, for God spoke the things we see into existence at some point in the past. To achieve future or present results, we need to "create" them by Faith. Thus, with Faith, we can bring into reality the unseen realities. These could include healing for the bodies, acquiring new opportunities in business, employment, or enterprise, or gaining new favors and abundant blessings. You don't need Faith for what you currently have and see; you need Faith for the achievements and accomplishments you need or want in your near or distant future. Faith is for what you desire to have or will succeed in next.

Related Prayer

Dear Heavenly Father,

Give us faith, nothing but holy faith, Lord;
So, we can believe in the promises of our God;
In those things eyes and reason cannot reach;
And in lessons lofty, senses cannot teach.

In the name of Christ Jesus, our Lord,
Amen.

5 | VICARIOUS VICTORY

*"Yet in all these things we are more than
conquerors through Him who loved us,"
(Romans 8:37 – NKJV);*

*"But thanks be to God, who gives us the victory
through our Lord Jesus Christ," (1 Corinthians
15:57, ESV).*

Introduction:

In the Law of Torts, in civil and
employment settings, an employer may be
vicariously liable. The employer succumbs
to vicarious liability for the misdeeds of their
employee if that misdeed was committed by the
employee or agent in the course of her
employment. A similar event happens in
Christianity. Christ Jesus won a victory against
evil and the devil. The accruements of this
victory are bequeathed directly upon those who
neither fought in the battle nor deserved the
victory. Victory was given to those who

offended (sinned) as a reward for their acknowledgment of the victory. In this sermon, we will consider three points: Victory completed; villain defeated; and vassals seated. The three points will be discussed in that order, and a conclusion and application will be drawn. Then a related prayer will be offered.

1. Victory Completed

Battles don't determine the end of conflicts. Because it is possible to win a battle and still lose the war. What determines victory is the completion of the war. The enemy surrenders or is captured and their instruments of war are captured or destroyed. The war between Satan and God was centered on one issue: Returning the original authority man had back to man. That authority had been usurped by Satan when he used a subtle serpent to lure humanity into disobedience. Man succumbed, sold inheritance to the devil, and harvested death and Hell.

"But when [in God's plan] the proper time had fully come, God sent His Son, born of a woman, born under the [regulations of the] Law, so that He might redeem and liberate those who were under the Law, that we [who believe] might be adopted as sons [as God's children with all rights as fully grown members of a family]."[49] The operative word is "redeem,"

---

[49] Galatians 4:4-5, AV

from where we derive the concept of redemption.

Redemption is defined as, "The action of regaining or gaining possession of something in exchange for payment or clearing a debt."[50] God, through Christ's own blood, repaid the debt we owed Satan because of sin. And then, without forfeiting the victory, Christ died and rose again from the dead. If He had not risen, there would be no salvation: "And if Christ has not been raised, your faith doesn't mean anything."[51] In other words, Christ's sinlessness, His message, His life, His death, would mean nothing if He had not risen. His resurrection completed the victory.

2. Villain Defeated

In Christ dying for us, God demonstrated His true love for us (for scarcely a good man dies for another good man, but for a Righteous Man to have died for sinners, that is true and great love). But in resurrecting, Christ retook all authority and power from the devil. Christ has given that authority back to man: "Look, I have given you authority over all the power of the enemy..."[52]

---

[50] From Oxford Languages online
[51] 1 Corinthians 15, NIRV
[52] Luke 10:19, NLT

Here lies ultimate victory. Power and authority are not the same things. Surely, Satan has power. We see it in the infliction of disease (Covid-19, for example), in his presiding over death, his malicious imposition of misery through hate and wars, his procurement of men's souls for his own aggrandizement, and his unsolicited abuse of human bodies and wills, and so on. However, the province of authority belongs to believers in Christ.

Thus, we have, "authority over all the power of the enemy." We acquired this authority vicariously, when we believed in the completed work of redemption of Christ. We have conquered in a war we didn't fight; and we have accumulated the trophies of the battle in which we didn't shed a single drop of blood. So, we are more than conquerors – because conquerors participate in a war; we did not.

Man (humanity) lost power to Satan through disobedience. Man (Jesus) grabbed back authority over the devil through obedience: "For just as through the disobedience of the one man the many were made sinners, so also through the obedience of the one man the many will be made righteous."[53] As we obey God, we also acquire the power to "crush Satan under [our] feet."[54]

---

[53] Romans 5:19, NIV
[54] Romans 16:20, ERV

Our victory is through Christ, and through Him alone.[55] We win each battle we participate in, because we do so through Christ Jesus. Our victory is only certain through Christ. Without Christ, we have lost every spiritual battle we engage in, even before we fight. Because our war is not worldly; our weapons are not carnal.[56]

That is also why we pray "in the name of Jesus"; because we are nothing without Him. We know that if we pray or war against evil in our own strength, we come up short. Christ Himself said that in His name, believers shall have authority (and power) over devils, and they shall sharpen their tongues to welcome favor and blessings.[57]

3. Vassals Seated

In international warfare and relations, vassal states are those that hold land by feudal tenure on conditions of homage (worship) and allegiance (submission), usually to a superior or victorious state.[58] This is the message of Grace, that us, who once had no name, no nation, and no identity, have been elevated to sit with Christ in the heavenly places: "Blessed be the God and Father of our Lord Jesus Christ, who has

---

[55] 1 Corinthians 15:57, *supra.*

[56] See 2 Corinthians 10:4

[57] See Mark 16:17

[58] See Oxford Languages online, *supra.*

blessed us in Christ with every spiritual blessing in the Heavenly realms."[59]

In other words, vassals have, ironically, become victors. This has given believers tremendous privileges. Believers in Christ will judge this world, this life, and angels (in the world to come): "Do you not know that the saints will judge the world? And if you are to judge the world, are you not competent to judge trivial cases? Do you not know that we will judge angels? How much more the things of this life!"[60]

And according to Peter, believers in Christ are a chosen people, a royal priesthood, a holy nation, God's special possession, and God-worshippers.[61] At His glorious feast, it is not the powerful, the renown, or the deserved who are seated; it is vassals (whomsoever believes) who is seated.

---

[59] Ephesians 1:3, Berean Study Bible (BSB)
[60] 1 Corinthians 6:2-3, BSB
[61] See 1 Peter 2:9

Conclusion & Application

"In Christ," that phrase, should not just be a cliché; it is everything you need for victory and sustenance. You are guaranteed victory in and for everything you do or say in the name of Christ. This means, in essence, that if Christ Jesus can have victory, if you claim it in His name, that victory is yours as well. All you need is to trust Him through faith. Your victory in life is sure and amen in Christ. If you are experiencing spiritual defeats, it might mean that you are either not laying claim to Christ's victory or you are defaulting in faith. Believe in Him, child of God, and all His victories are yours. In Christ, we have, do, and, in fact, enjoy vicarious victory.

Related Prayer

Oh, Lord, Great Father of all a good thing;
Our immortal, eternal, and Sovereign King;
In Christ, resides the fullness of the Godhead;
In Him, all is due, through the blood He shed.

In the name of Jesus, our Lord,
Amen.

6 | CONTRACTUAL CONSIDERATION

For the Kingdom of Heaven is like a landowner who went out early in the morning to hire men to work in his vineyard. He agreed to pay them a denarius for the day and sent them into his vineyard. About the third hour he went out and saw others standing in the marketplace doing nothing. He told them, "You also go and work in my vineyard, and I will pay you whatever is right." So, they went. He went out again about the sixth hour and the ninth hour and did the same thing. About the eleventh hour he went out and found still others standing around. He asked them, "Why have you been standing here all day long doing nothing?" "Because no one has hired us," they answered. He said to them, "You also go and work in my vineyard." When evening came, the owner of the vineyard said to his foreman, "Call the workers and pay them their wages, beginning with the last ones hired and going on to the first." The workers who were hired about the eleventh hour came and each received a denarius. So, when those came who were hired first, they expected to receive more. But each one of them also received a denarius. When they received it, they began to grumble against the landowner. "These men who were hired last worked only one hour," they said, "and you have made them equal to us who have borne the burden of the work and the heat of the day." But he answered one of them, "Friend, I am not being unfair to you. Didn't you agree to work for a denarius? Take your pay and go." (Matthew 20: 1-14).

Introduction

In this sermon, we consider the true meaning of divine apportionment by drawing from the common-law principles of contract law. In law, generally, a valid contract should have at least three binding elements. These elements are an offer, acceptance, and consideration. (Other factors, such as capacity, the meeting of minds or *consensus ad idem*, formality and legality, are presumed, at least for the purposes of this discourse).

The central thesis of this sermon is consideration, and the idea that consideration need not be adequate or sufficient. In short, once an agreement has been made as to *quantum* (amount), its value is irrelevant. To develop this thesis further, the following points have been identified: Offer accepted; consideration expected; and contract respected. The points will be dealt with in the above-mentioned order, before a conclusive application and a related prayer are offered.

1. Offer Accepted

Just like in legal contracts, an offeror makes an offer to the offeree. In the Bible passage under discussion, our Lord, made an offer to five sets of people at five different hour-periods for the consideration of "a denarius for the day." Once an offer has been made and accepted, the adequacy of consideration is not an issue for the Courts.

This principle has been respected for generations upon generations. What the Courts respect is what was agreed upon, and not the value of what was agreed to.

In our case scenario, one group began work, say, at 6:00 a.m., another at 9:00 a.m., another at 12:00 p.m., and yet another at 3:00 p.m. The last group agreed to begin work, say, at 11:00 p.m., with only an hour remaining before the end of the day. All the groups agreed to be paid a denarius[62] for the day. At the point of contract, all the groups accepted the offer. The Bible says, "Yet to all who did receive Him, to those who believed in His name, He gave the right to

---

[62] Probably $2 worth in those days

become children of God."[63] The word, "receive," means to accept. We find a similar injunction: "For God so loved the world that He gave His one and only Son, that whoever believes in Him shall not perish but have eternal life."[64] Those who will enter the Kingdom of God, have accepted the offer God gave, that of His Son.[65]

2. Consideration Expected

In contract law, consideration is anything of value that is exchanged between parties in a contractual negotiation. It can be any amount, of any value. Consideration itself does not need to be sufficient, what is sufficient is the fact that the parties, willingly and without coercion, agreed to the exchange.[66] In our story under review, all the five sets of individuals accepted our Lord's offer, volitionally, and agreed to its terms, unequivocally. Specifically, they all agreed to a denarius for the day, no matter how many hours they worked in that day.

---

[63] John 1:12

[64] John 3:16

[65] See John 3:3

[66] In law, undue influence, unconscionability, fraudulent misrepresentation, or duress, may render contract void ab initio (defective or of no legal effect from the beginning).

In Christianity, we entered into a special contract with God called a Covenant. As indicated before, a valid contract must have at least three elements of offer, acceptance, and consideration. In our covenant with God, offer and acceptance are required. However, only God gave consideration – His only begotten Son, and we gave Him nothing of value in return. It is still a contract based on an exception in law called a contract under seal. An agreement without consideration is known as a gratuity or gratuitous promise. When a gratuity is offered and accepted under seal, it becomes enforceable at law as a contract.

The new covenant was contracted and sealed in three steps. First, Jesus Christ secured redemption by means of His own blood.[67] Second, Jesus Himself became a seal approved by God: "For on [Jesus] God the Father has set his seal."[68] And third, those who accept Jesus are sealed with the Holy Spirit as guarantee: "And you also were included in Christ when you heard the message of truth, the gospel of your salvation. When you believed, you were marked in him with a seal, the promised Holy Spirit."[69]

---

[67] Hebrews 9:11-15
[68] John 6:27
[69] Ephesians 1:13

Thus, even without humanity's providing a valid consideration, God sealed the agreement, and in that act, He also transformed what would have been a mere gratuitous promise into a valid contract. And this is the basis of God's promises to us – they will always be fulfilled – because they are based on an eternal contract: "For no matter how many promises God has made, they are 'Yes' in Christ. And so, through him the 'Amen' is spoken by us to the glory of God."[70]

3. Contract Respected

Our belief in the Lord Jesus is rewardable. In other words, we do not enter into a contract with God without consideration. God will reward the fact that we accepted His offer of salvation and redemption, and their accompanying rewards. The rewards vary, and they range from mundane, to heavenly glory, and to eternal life. There is a reward of answered prayer.[71] Those who give or are generous or hospitable, will be rewarded with a good and expansive measure.[72] The reward of a ticket into the Kingdom of God.[73] In addition, there is a great reward in heaven for those who suffer or go through trials for the sake and name of Christ and truth; for those who love and pray

---

[70] 2 Corinthians 1:20
[71] Matthew 6:6
[72] Luke 6:38; Luke 14:12-14
[73] Matthew 25:20-23, 37-40

for their enemies; or those who endure in ministry.[74] There is a reward for quality work, for both earthly employers and our Heavenly Father.[75] Moreover, there are five crowns available for those who accepted God's covenant of love. There is a crown that never perishes.[76] A crown of rejoicing.[77] A crown of righteousness.[78] A crown of glory.[79] And finally, a crown of life.[80]

Implicit in the Bible, is the adherence to common-law principles of consideration, even in the final analysis. For example, the Bible says, "For the Son of Man is going to come in the glory of His Father with His angels and will then repay every man according to his deeds.[81]

God will not give rewards equally; He will award each person a reward with equity and fairness.[82] This is what in our passage is referred to as, "I am not being unfair to you." The degree of

---

[74] Luke 6:22-23, 35; 2 Corinthians 4:17-18; 1 Peter 1:6-7; 2 John 1:7-8

[75] Colossians 3:23-24; 1 Corinthians 3:11-14; 1 Corinthians 3:8; 2 Corinthians 9:6

[76] 1 Corinthians 9:24-25

[77] 1 Thessalonians 2:19

[78] 2 Timothy 4:8

[79] 1 Peter 5:4

[80] Revelation 2:10

[81] Matthew 16:27

[82] The concept of equity stands on the assumption of fairness. Equality stands on the position that all, regardless of value brought forward, are rewarded the similarly.

fairness is based on the gift each person received and what they did with it. Some, indeed, will escape with a whisker – those people will, surely, enter into the Kingdom of Heaven, but without other rewards or crowns. Those who put their gifts to good use here on earth, will have their rewards multiplied. Our value on earth is tied to our purpose; once we discharge our purpose here on earth, death is a welcome partner: "Now when David had served God's purpose in his own generation, he fell asleep."[83]

Conclusion & Application

There is a misconception that every believer will receive the same reward. The truth is, everyone who believes in Jesus and accepts the free gift of eternal life, is, and will be, saved. However, salvation is merely the entry point. What you do with the degree of grace God has given to you, is very important. If you sit on potential or neglect your gifts, abilities, and talents, you will not receive the same reward as those who invested into their gifts. Remember that your gift is to the world – not to a church or a congregation. Pastors, evangelists, teachers, prophets, and apostles are the gift to the church.

Every believer in Christ is a gift to the world. Their singing, writing, dancing, politicking,

---

[83] Acts 13:36

accounting, leadership, parenting, making money, and etc., are all respective gifts to the world.

You will not receive rewards for what you will do in heaven, only for what you did on earth. As the writer to the Hebrews admonishes: "Therefore let us leave the elementary teachings about Christ and go on to maturity, not laying again the foundation of repentance from dead works, and of faith in God, instruction about baptisms, the laying on of hands, the resurrection of the dead, and eternal judgment."[84] Repentance, faith, baptisms, laying on of hands, resurrection, and judgment, are all elementary concepts. In other words, they are for spiritual primary school. Most churches preach these, week after week, year after year, thereby creating spiritually immature believers.

Move on – participate in politics, learn a trade, reach out to the vulnerable, create jobs, invent money-making ventures, write poetry, publish books, discover ideas and technology, change courses of history, leave behind legacies, and etc., with the gifts God has given you. Here on earth, you shall be fulfilled, and in heaven, great shall be your reward.

---

[84] Hebrews 6:1-2

Related Prayer

Oh, Lord, our Father, grant us grace to
overcome lethargy;
But for great exploits here on earth, grant us
authentic energy;
Thank you, Lord Jesus, Thy blood has made all
things new;
Thy seal, Spirit, spur our works, in quantity,
and quality, too.

In the name of Jesus, our Lord,
Amen.

7 | THE NEIGHBOR PRINCIPLE

*But wanting to justify himself, he asked Jesus,
"And who is my neighbor?" Jesus took up this
question and said, "A man was going down from
Jerusalem to Jericho when he fell into the hands of
robbers. They stripped him, beat him, and went
away, leaving him half dead. Now by chance a
priest was going down the same road, but when
he saw him, he passed by on the other side. So
too, when a Levite came to that spot and saw
him, he passed by on the other side. But when a
Samaritan on a journey came upon him, he
looked at him and had compassion. He went to
him and bandaged his wounds, pouring on oil
and wine. Then he put him on his own animal,
brought him to an inn, and took care of him.
The next day he took out two denarii and gave
them to the innkeeper. "Take care of him," he
said, "and on my return I will repay you for any
additional expense." Which of these three do you
think was a neighbor to the man who fell into the
hands of robbers?" "The one who showed him*

mercy," replied the expert in the law. Then Jesus
told him, "Go and do likewise,"
(Luke 10: 29-37).

Introduction

Our Lord expounded on the Neighbor Principle long before Lord Atkin established its *ratio* in the case of *Donoghue v Stevenson*[85] in England in 1932. This was an appeal by the plaintiff, Mrs. May Donoghue, to the House of Lords in England. The action was to recover damages for illness she suffered as the outcome of consuming the contents of rotten remains of a snail in a bottle of ginger-beer.

On August 26th, 1928, Donoghue met a friend, Mabel Hannah, who bought her a ginger beer from Wellmeadow Cafe in Paisley. After consuming most of the contents of the bottle of ginger-beer, she discovered the said remains of a grossly decomposed snail that floated out of the bottle while being poured into her tumbler.

The bottle was made of dark opaque glass which made it impossible for her to notice the snail inside. This caused her to suffer from shock and severe gastroenteritis. She took legal action against Mr. Stevenson. She could not sue Stevenson for breach of contract as she herself

---

[85] [1932] AC 562

did not purchase the drink; she was not a party to it.

It could be improbable to prove that Stevenson owed her a duty of care. It was unlikely that Stevenson had known that he had sold a flawed product. It could be true that Stevenson did not know that his product had been sold, either. Donoghue's lawyer maintained that Stevenson owed a duty to his consumers to take reasonable care to guarantee that his product was safe for everyone's consumption. She was successful in the appeal with three majority and two dissents.

In this sermon, we link Lord Atkin's redefinition of the "neighbor" to our Lord's Golden Rule – treating neighbors as we would like to be treated. The following three points will be used: Neighbor principle; neighbor proximity; and neighbor priority. The points will be discussed in that order before a conclusive application is drawn and a related prayer is offered.

1. The Neighbor Principle

A self-righteous lawyer came to Jesus and asked a fundamentally relevant question: "And who is my neighbor?" Our Lord responded through a hypothetical allegory we have come to dub, "The Parable of the Good Samaritan." Christ lays out the rationale with both Jewish priest and Levite who ignore social and moral etiquette while a Samaritan offers help.

Samaritans were viewed as hostile, evil and bad. The Jews believed that the Samaritans were responsible for harassing Jewish pilgrims, scattering human bones, and even labeled them as pagan Assyrians.

To the Jews, Samaritans were far away from the conception of a neighbor, let alone a good neighbor. Alienated by both racial and cultural bigotry, a Samaritan, in the story, is not deterred to render a good deed to a wanting Jew. This was game changer.

To a Jew pondering on this story at the time, it was *anathema*, unheard of, and even unattainable. What a priest and a Levite did could even be celebrated in those days; it was justifiable.

However, our Lord Jesus Christ shows that good neighborliness does not depend on race, tribe, culture, or social definition. It is a matter of conviction and conscience. To Christ, any and everyone in trouble, distress, danger or need, is a neighbor.

Christ's postulation on the Neighbor Principle may seem reactionary at first, until one situates it into the Golden Rule Theorem. The Golden Rule was first articulated several years before Christ. In the Old Testament, it is written:

"Thou shalt not avenge, nor bear any grudge against the children of thy people, but thou shalt love thy neighbor as thyself: I am the LORD."[86]

Thus, the Golden Rule was the architect of the Neighbor Principle. Christ refined it further in the New Testament: "So whatever you wish that others would do to you, do also to them, for this is the Law and the Prophets."[87] The foundation of the law is established on this principle. The teachings and preaching of the prophets were as well founded on the same principle.

What Lord Atkin did in the famous *Donoghue* case, was to extend the principle further in a proactive sense. In other words, the Judge was applying the principle to current and future harm that may obtain as a result of the violation of this principle.

The learned judge opined, "The rule that you are to love your neighbor becomes in law, you must not injure your neighbor; and the lawyer's question, who is my neighbor? …. The answer seems to be persons who are so closely and directly affected by my act that I ought reasonably to have them in contemplation as being so affected when I am directing my mind to the acts or omissions which are called in question."[88] Thus, the Bible defined the

---

[86] Leviticus 19:18
[87] Matthew 7:12
[88] *Donoghue, supra.*

Neighbor Principle, and English law applied it to real human situations.

2. Neighbor Proximity

In the Bible as well as in English law, what is central to the Neighbor Principle is the idea of proximity. A neighbor is one close enough, both in terms physical closeness and a state of proximity. It can be said that a neighbor is anyone who may be harmed by another's action or omission.

Christ asserts a self-introspective question in the Golden Rule, thus, an action that may harm oneself should not be contemplated on somebody else. That somebody else, is the neighbor. The efficacy of this principle is covenantal; in the absence of a social contract, there is a rule of nature that fixes and requires humans to treat each other with care and love. In law, this binding force is known as a Duty of Care.

Apostle Paul further redefines the similitude of the law of nations (legal principles) with divine law (moral canon). The instructive apostle charges: "Let no debt remain outstanding, except the continuing debt to love one another, for whoever loves others has fulfilled the law."[89]

---

[89] Romans 13:8

characteristic. Faith is spiritual, but it always manifests socially. Jesus said: "When did we see You sick or in prison and visit You?' And the King will reply, 'Truly I tell you, whatever you did for one of the least of these brothers of Mine, you did for Me.' Then He will say to those on His left, 'Depart from Me, you who are cursed, into the eternal fire prepared for the devil and his angels.'"[94] Your faith or belief system is useless if it does not love or care for those around it. James put it this way, "Religion that God our Father accepts as pure and faultless is this: to look after orphans and widows in their distress and to keep oneself from being polluted by the world."[95] True faith and religion do good deeds. James is again on point: "But someone will say, 'You have faith; I have deeds.' Show me your faith without deeds, and I will show you my faith by my deeds."[96] And the culminating Scripture is captured in these words: "Love does no harm to a neighbor. Therefore, love is the fulfillment of the law."[97] In this regard, God's law and English law find commonness. So, go on, reflect on this and be a good neighbor to all humanity – one next person to you at a time.

---

[94] Matthew 25:39-41
[95] James 1:27
[96] James 2:18
[97] Romans 13:10

Related Prayer

Dear Heavenly Father, hear us as we pray for
humanity;
That love, care and amity should define true
Christianity;
Do create in us a sense that all around us, is a
neighbor;
And that here on earth, it should not be in
vain, our labor.

In the name of Jesus, our Lord,
Amen.

8 | READING THE LAW & SCRIPTURE

One day an expert in the law stood up to test Him. "Teacher," he asked, "What must I do to inherit eternal life?" "What is written in the Law?" Jesus replied. "How do you read it?" He answered, "'Love the Lord your God with all your heart and with all your soul and with all your strength and with all your mind' and 'Love your neighbor as yourself.'" "You have answered correctly," Jesus said. "Do this and you will live," (Luke 10:25-28).

Introduction

"How do you read it?" And not just what or why we read the Bible is important. Under the common-law system, at the heart of justice, law, and truth, are the rules of construction known as statutory interpretation. Similarly, at the heart of the discovery of truth in the Bible is scriptural interpretation. Both are the methods of investigation of truth. And in this sermon, we will highlight the purpose of scriptural interpretation by drawing upon three rules of statutory interpretation, namely: Mischief rule; plain meaning rule; and golden rule. The points will be dealt with in that order before a conclusive application is drawn, followed by a related prayer.

1. Mischief Rule

The mischief is the gap existing before the law and after it was passed. The role of the judge is to discover the mischief the legislature intended to cover by enacting the particular statute. The *Heydon's Case*[98] is cited as the first case to set a precedent on mischief rule of judicial statutory interpretation. It set a four-prong test, as follows: What the common-law was before enacting the statute; what mischief and defect were for which the common-law had been provided; the remedy Parliament had intended to resolve; and the true reason for the remedy.

Christ has pointed out the mischief that Scriptures intended to discover or the gap it intended to fill; all scriptures point to Jesus:

---

[98] (1584) 76 ER 637

"You search the Scriptures because you think they give you eternal life. But the Scriptures point to me!"[99] Christ does not dispute that Scriptures contain eternal life. He merely clarifies that eternal life is in Him. Indeed, Scriptures point to Christ who is both eternal life and the source of it. Answering the expert in the law, Christ points to Himself as the possessor and granter of eternal life. The greatest commandment, therefore, can be summed up as loving Jesus. And this is illustrative as: "Whoever has my commands and keeps them is the one who loves me. The one who loves me will be loved by my Father, and I too will love them and show myself to them."[100]

Mere stating that one loves Jesus or God is not enough, one should do the will of Jesus or God: "Not everyone who says to me, 'Lord, Lord,' will enter the kingdom of Heaven, but only the one who does the will of my Father who is in Heaven."[101] Jesus, is the link between the old law and the new covenant. Just like a Judge has to suppress a mischief and advance a remedy through the rules of construction, a diligent believer needs to dig deeper than simply browsing on what is written. The deeper one digs in Scripture, the better the chances of discovering the truth – which is Christ. Indeed, Christ is the remedy for sin and damnation.

---

[99] John 5:39
[100] John 14:21
[101] Matthew 7:21

2. Plain Meaning Rule

Merriam-Webster online dictionary defines the Plain Meaning Rule as, "A rule in statute or contract interpretation: when the language is unambiguous and clear on its face the meaning of the statute or contract must be determined from the language of the statute or contract and not from extrinsic evidence."[102]

To utilize this rule, the text is key – justice must be done in understanding the text itself without any external assistance, such as using a concordance or dictionary. After Paul and Silas preached, the Bereans went back and re-examined the texts to unlock what Paul and Silas preached: "And the people of Berea were more open-minded than those in Thessalonica, and they listened eagerly to Paul's message. They searched the Scriptures day after day to see if Paul and Silas were teaching the truth."[103]

The Plain Meaning Rule is enshrined in a hermeneutical device of scripture interpreting scripture, just like one statutory provision may be used to interpret another provision. Pete Lange writes: "So, what do we really mean when we say, 'Scripture interprets Scripture?' In short, it means that as we engage in hermeneutics (the art of interpretation), we interpret the implicit

---

[102] https://www.merriam-webster.com/ (assessed on February 16th, 2021)
[103] Acts 17:11

by the explicit and the cloudy through the clear."[104]

3. The Golden Rule

The golden rule of statutory interpretation was defined in the *Adamson Case*, wherein it could be applied where an application of the literal rule would lead to an absurdity. The Courts may then apply a secondary meaning.[105]

When mere mechanical and grammatical meaning of words in a statute may not be sufficient to secure justice, Courts often modify the literal rules in order to cure the ambiguity and absurdity. This may also be construed as contextual analysis of the statute. Words require context to be understood. Context may be what existed during the enactment process.

The Golden Rule may be relevant to biblical and scriptural interpretation. However, caution must be had in view of the restriction offered in the Bible: "Above all, you must understand that no prophecy of Scripture came about by the prophet's own interpretation of things."[106]

---

[104] Pete Lange, "Scripture Interprets Scripture: What Does this Mean?" 1517.org, June 24th, 2020
[105] *River Wear Commissioners v Adamson*, (1876-77) L.R. 2 App Cas 743.
[106] 2 Peter 1:20

Indeed, certain events and concepts that may require interpretation may not have existed when the Bible was written. In those circumstances the Golden Rule may come handy. The caveat always lies in overstretching or under-stretching the principles.

Issues of contemporary nuances such as abortion, same-sex marriage, technology, and even practices like tithing which existed in the agrarian economy, may be dealt with using the Golden Rule.

And the golden authority for such is in this verse, "All Scripture is God-breathed and is useful for teaching, rebuking, correcting, and training in righteousness…"[107] Thus, the inspiration that is inherent in Scriptures is necessary to the correct interpretation of the Word of God.

In 1938, John Willis published an article called, "Statutory Interpretation in a Nutshell"?[108] In that article, Willis asserts, "Although judges purport to apply them, in fact outcomes are determined by the politics and arbitrary preferences of the presiding judge."[109]

This is in reaction to the realistic view of legal philosophizing. However, a truth that should

---

[107] 2 Timothy 3:16
[108] (1939) 16 Can. Bar Rev. 1
[109] *Ibid.*

not be overlooked is in the limitation imposed on temporal exegesis, both in legal courts and in the church.

In law, two philosophies have emerged, positivism and judicial interventionism. The former is an approach to the interpretation of law that states that the meaning to be given to the words in legal rules should be the ordinary, dictionary meaning without resorting to social, economic, or political values to aid in interpretation.

And the later is an approach to the interpretation of law that draws on social, economic, and political values in interpreting the meaning and application of legal rules and principles.

Lying in between these two schools of thought, truth may be lost, sacrificed, or even averted. It is for this reason that in scriptural interpretation, emphasis should be had to the Spirit's inspiration and instruction. Many are the times, being human, judges have acquitted the guilty, and even punished the innocent.

If this is taken into scriptural distinctions, it might mean misleading the church into false doctrines and misplaced interpretations of God's Word, leading to serious eternal consequences, such as loss of heaven or fall from grace.[110]

Christ never shunned the efficacy of the Scripture, both in the Old and New testaments: "Do not think that I have come to abolish the Law or the Prophets; I have not come to abolish them but to fulfill them."[111] And, indeed, "He is before all things, and in him all things hold together."[112]

Conclusion & Application

Those who preach or judge have a very high burden placed upon them. They have both the power and opportunity to interpret the Scripture and the law, respectively.

Both the Scripture and the law contain the truth, but this can be missed or even abused. Because of this weakness, both those who are lawyering before judicial magistrates and those who listen to sermons must exercise due diligence in searching the truth.

The burden is not only on those who judge or preach, but also on those who are judged (through their lawyers) and those who listen to

---

[110] See Galatians 5:4. The concept of "Falling from Grace" is comprehensively explained in Mwewa, *Law & Grace, supra.*, from page 50
[111] Matthew 5:17
[112] Colossians 1:17

sermons to making sure that they have done their duty in searching the truth through the law and Scripture, respectively.

The deceiver and the deceived will both be punished. This is what is meant by the verses, "Not many of you should become teachers, my fellow believers, because you know that we who teach will be judged more strictly,"[113] and "My people are destroyed from lack of knowledge."[114] You read your Bible and listen to your pastors, but Jesus asks, "How do you read it?"

---

[113] James 3:1
[114] Hosea 4:6

Related Prayer

Dear Heavenly Father,

There are wolves in sheep's clothing, Oh,
Lord, show us;
It's only in the full revelation, the full
knowledge of Jesus;
That our safety and security clearly fit into
divine glory;
May we not be dupes of Satan's machinations
and gory.

In the name of Jesus, our Lord,
Amen.

9 | DIVINE DISPUTE RESOLUTION

"For, there is one God and one Mediator who can reconcile God and humanity—the man Christ Jesus," (1 Timothy 2:5).

Introduction

I n the barbaric earlier centuries, people resolved conflicts through barbaric means. The first mechanism known to humanity for conflict resolution was war. Thus, from the Bible (and even in the Quran), we find this method sanctioned and even promoted. During what is known as the renaissance, improvements in knowledge and human dignity, led to the prioritization of resolving conflicts by trials, also known as litigation.

Recently, the world has embraced an ancient method, referenced in the Bible as mediation. War is said to be power-based, litigation is right's based, but mediation is interest-based. Arguably, the best mechanism for resolving conflict is a sister-mechanism to mediation known as negotiation.

However, for divine redemption, it was nearly impossible to arbitrate negotiation because humanity had no standing before God; man could not buy his way out of sin. God found a mediator through the human person of His Son, Jesus Christ.

In this sermon, we consider three points: Mediation impossible without Christ; mediation implausible without a covenant; and mediation possible with a sinless human conciliator. The points will be discussed beginning with mediation implausible without a covenant, followed by the other points in their respective order before a conclusive application and a related prayer are made.

1. Mediation Implausible without a Covenant

It is grossly erroneous to think that human beings invented the "Rule of Law." It was neither jurists nor politicians who introduced the Rule of Law to governance, God did. Isaiah had written long before Christ that God is a government, with all the three divisions of power in One person: "For the LORD is our judge, the LORD is our lawgiver, the LORD is our king; it is he who will save us."[115]

In fact, this verse introduces four branches of government: Judiciary ("judge"); Legislature ("lawgiver"); Executive ("king"); and Commander-in-Chief ("it is he who will save us"). From the beginning, God intended to lead the Hebrew nation in this fashion, where only God was the government. But the Hebrew leaders rebelled and sought for a king just like all other nations: "So all the elders of Israel gathered together and came to Samuel at Ramah. They said to him, 'You are old, and your sons do not walk in your ways; now appoint a king to lead us, such as all the other nations have.'"[116]

The mistake the Hebrew nation made was to choose a leader based on physical characteristics: "Kish had a son named Saul, as handsome a young man as could be found anywhere in Israel, and he was a head taller than anyone else."[117] They went for a good-looking and tallest boy. And this has been the weakness of human judgment; it equates intelligence, power and skill to outward looks. But God had already warned the Hebrew nation:

---

[115] Isaiah 33:22
[116] I Samuel 8:4-5
[117] 1 Samuel 9:2

> This is what the king who will reign over you will do: He will take your sons and make them serve with his chariots and horses, and they will run in front of his chariots. Some he will assign to be commanders of thousands and commanders of fifties, and others to plow his ground and reap his harvest, and still others to make weapons of war and equipment for his chariots. He will take your daughters to be perfumers and cooks and bakers. He will take the best of your fields and vineyards and olive groves and give them to his attendants. He will take a tenth of your grain and of your vintage and give it to his officials and attendants. Your menservants and maidservants and the best of your cattle and donkeys he will take for his own use. He will take a tenth of your flocks, and you yourselves will become his slaves. When that day comes, you will cry out for relief from the king you have chosen, and the LORD will not answer you in that day.[118]

These are the characteristics of a ruler who has no regard for man and who does not fear God or respect the law: He considers citizens his servants; he makes the citizens his shield (he leads from behind); he uses girls and women as his sex toys; he grabs the land and uses it for personal benefit; he imposes exorbitant taxes and tariffs in order to enrich himself and his family; he never listens to people, no matter how loud they cry.

He is also corrupt, perverter of justice and acts like a demagogue: "They turned aside after

---

[118] See 1 Samuel 8, *infra*.

dishonest gain and accepted bribes and perverted justice."[119]

And the reason humans make this mistake is because they do not look at the heart: "But the LORD said to Samuel, 'Do not consider his appearance or his height, for I have rejected him. The LORD does not look at the things people look at. People look at the outward appearance, but the LORD looks at the heart.'"[120]

It takes discernment to elect a leader who will rule with justice, empathy and sound judgment. And God eventually chose David – young, unassuming and even despised – to become His own man after His heart.[121]

To govern, one needs a social contract with the people. In almost all civilized societies, that social contract is achieved via constitutions which mandate for free and fair elections. The people, thus, transact a contract with the elected or appointed leaders to rule on oath to the constitution.

God, the quintessential jurist, does the same. Before He governs a people, He first enters into an agreement with them. This agreement is known as a covenant. The first covenant God had with the Hebrew nation was defective; it

---

[119] 1 Samuel 8:3
[120] 1 Samuel 16:7
[121] See 1 Samuel 13:14 and Acts 13:22

had been tainted by sin. God wanted to find a man (holy, blameless and sinless) to enter with him into a new covenant. But "for all [had] sinned and [fallen] short of the glory of God."[122] God had no other option, but to become such a Man. So, He "became flesh and made his dwelling among us. We have seen his glory, the glory of the one and only Son, who came from the Father, full of grace and truth."[123]

And not only that, "He made himself nothing by taking the very nature of a servant, being made in human likeness."[124] In this state, as Man (on behalf of men), God had finally found a Man with whom He could enter into a covenant.

That permanent agreement was covenanted through blood: "This is my blood of the covenant, which is poured out for many for the forgiveness of sins."[125] In this New Covenant, God on one side and us (through Christ) on the other, sin had permanently been dealt with. It restored the once *paradise lost* into a new Heaven gained. And as a human High Priest (who came in the order of Melchizedek),[126] Christ "did not enter by means of the blood of goats and calves; but he entered the Most Holy Place once for all by his own blood, thus obtaining eternal

---

[122] Romans 3:23

[123] John 1:14

[124] Philippians 2:7

[125] Matthew 26:28

[126] See Hebrews 5:6

redemption."[127] Our freedom (redemption) is completed; it is permanent.

Christ has achieved the impossible. First, there was no human who was sinless; Christ became one. Second, in one stroke, Christ became both the representative Man, and also the mediator to link God with men.

Remember that even in our own legal traditions, there is no need for a mediator unless there is more than one party involved in a dispute. The Bible is clear on this, too: "A mediator is unnecessary, however, for only one party; but God is one."[128] Christ stands as a mediator for two parties – God and us.

2. Mediation Impossible without Christ

Christ plays a role not found in human mediation mechanisms. He is the only one who qualifies to mediate in this redemption story. In the English legal system, it is generally understood that one cannot be both a mediator and a witness in the same matter.

The reason is because of avoiding conflict of interest and a reasonable apprehension of bias. A mediator by definition is a go-between, that is, an internunciator, or a reconciler. Total

---

[127] Hebrews 9:12
[128] Galatians 3:20

independence and impartiality are required for the mediation to have any pursuance.

However, Christ's mediatorship has a special place. In legal mediation, the parties can choose a mediator together, or one party may choose a mediator. In case of where both parties mutually choose a mediator, both parties will bear the cost of mediation.

In situations where only one party chooses a mediator, the party which chose the mediator will bear the cost of mediation. Some mediations are statutory, and in those situations, the law would have apportioned who would bear the cost burden.

In some contractual mediation (akin to covenantal mediation), the terms of mediation would have been set in a contract.

A covenantal mediation is based on an exception to the rule. Because for a covenant to be binding, the stronger party must sign it under seal. In the divine mediation, God sponsored the mediation and accepted a payment through blood. Christ, is, therefore, able to both stand as mediator and witness but for different purposes.

He is a mediator to the covenant. In other words, He mediates the covenant: "Now, however, Jesus has received a much more excellent ministry, just as the covenant He mediates is better and is founded on better promises,"[129] and "…to Jesus the mediator of a new covenant, and to the sprinkled blood that speaks a better word than the blood of Abel."[130]

And Christ is the appointed arbiter of the New Covenant because of one quality earthly mediators do not possess; He died – thus, completed the process – and He rose again (resurrected) – thus, acquiring a new role altogether, that of a witness as well.

And the extent of mediation is in this wise: "Therefore, Christ is the mediator of a new covenant, so that those who are called may receive the promised eternal inheritance, now that He has died to redeem them from the transgressions committed under the first covenant."[131]

3. Mediation Possible with a Sinless Human Conciliator

In Christ, God achieved another feat, He reconciled us back to Him: "All this is from

---

[129] Hebrews 8:6
[130] Hebrews 12:24
[131] Hebrews 9:15

God, who reconciled us to Himself through Christ and gave us the ministry of reconciliation: that God was reconciling the world to Himself in Christ, not counting men's trespasses against them. And He has committed to us the message of reconciliation."[132]

Reconciliation is the process of re-uniting once enemies into friends. And this is also akin to State-sponsored conciliation: It was God who sponsored the reconciliation process using the only one who could represent man, Christ.

In that conciliation process, Christ has an added role, that of humanity's advocate or lawyer: "My little children, I am writing these things to you so that you will not sin. But if anyone does sin, we have an advocate before the Father--Jesus Christ, the Righteous One."[133]

Remember that what initially separated us from God and made us His enemy, was sin. Christ dealt with sin in redemption and as a conciliator, "He lives forever to intercede with God on their behalf."[134] In ancient times, God had lamented, "I looked for someone among them who would build up the wall and stand before me in the gap on behalf of the land so I would not have to destroy it, but I found no one."[135]

---

[132] 2 Corinthians 5:18-19
[133] 1 John 2:1
[134] Hebrews 7:25
[135] Ezekiel 22:30

But, thankfully, in the fullness of time, God found Christ, and we are the beneficiaries. Having redeemed us, God reconciled us back to Himself as friends: "For if, while we were God's enemies, we were reconciled to him through the death of his Son, how much more, having been reconciled, shall we be saved through his life!"[136] Reconciliation moved us from just being forgiven into being God's friends.

Then God did another feat unimaginable; He adopted us (reconciled as friends, then adopting us as His children) as sons: "For He chose us in Him before the foundation of the world to be holy and blameless in His presence. *In love* He predestined us for adoption as His sons through Jesus Christ, according to the good pleasure of His will, to the praise of His glorious grace, which He has freely given us in the Beloved One."[137] Adoption is more than just an act of grace; it is, primarily, an act of love.

Redemption is key to our salvation. But it came with added benefits. First reconciliation and then adoption. "But when the time had fully come, God sent His Son, born of a woman, born under the law, to redeem those under the law, that we might receive our adoption as sons. And because you are sons, God sent the Spirit of His Son into our hearts, crying out, 'Abba,

---

[136] Romans 5:10
[137] Ephesians 1:5 (emphasis added)

Father!'"[138] And with adoption, God has become our Father.

And even more beneficial, now we have an inheritance through Christ, because only children receive an inheritance from their fathers: "We have also received an inheritance in Christ."[139]

You see child of God; redemption was a legal act. Reconciliation is a political or social act. But adoption is a matter of the heart; it is love: "See what great love the Father has lavished on us, that we should be called children of God! And that is what we are!"[140] Henceforth, our relationship with God has become one of love, not of duty or convenience.

Conclusion & Application

When you hear someone say, "It is all because of Jesus Christ," it actually means just that. From redemption, to reconciliation, to adoption, it is all possible because of Christ. In redemption, sin is dealt with. In reconciliation, enmity is dealt with. And in adoption, we now have a Father.

---

[138] Galatians 4:5
[139] Ephesians 1:11
[140] 1 John 3:1

Of course, none of this happened perchance, God had predestined it to be so: "And those he predestined, he also called; those he called, he also justified; those he justified, he also glorified."[141]

In other words, we have inherited glory as God's children: "Now if we are children, then we are heirs – heirs of God and co-heirs with Christ, if indeed we share in his sufferings in order that we may also share in his glory."[142]

In Christ, our inheritance is sure – because Christ protects the proceeds of redemption by standing in three concurrent offices: As a mediator, witness and advocate. This feat cannot be achieved by anybody, except Him who firstly, lived, secondly, died, and thirdly, He lives again.

---

[141] Romans 8:30
[142]Romans 8:17

Related Prayer

Dear Heavenly Father,

How magnificent the wonder of this truth in
excelsior?
To redemption, add adoption to make us even
wealthier;
In glorious exultations of Thy legendary
effulgence;
Found in Thee, Abba, glorious is Thy gracious
indulgence;
Words do fail me, Almighty Sir, Oh, gracious
Creator;
And for Thee, Christ, my Lord, witness, and
mediator;
Be all the beauty, the flowers, the confetti and
flurries;
Be worshipped by all, Oh, Attorney of
attorneys.

In the name of Jesus, our Lord,
Amen.

10 | THE ADVOCACY OF CHRIST

"My dear children, I write this to you so that you
will not sin. But if anybody does sin, we have an
advocate with the Father--Jesus Christ, the
Righteous One," (1 John 2:1).

Introduction

Apostle John, in his old age, had come to understand the real meaning of love. He had also come to a critical realization that sinning is inevitable, but with good news. Those who sin have an advocate in the person of Jesus Christ. Jesus is humanity's quintessential lawyer – who stands before God pleading for their weaknesses and sins. He is able to make and resolve every case that is brought before the Father on behalf of the humans. Unlike human attorneys (also known as lawyers or advocates), Jesus is also a witness in their defence. He lived, died, and lives again. This, in essence, means that He can vouch for them as the one who took away their sins and presented the evidence of His own blood before His Father, whom the Scripture calls,

"The Great Judge." In this sermon, we consider the following three points: The nature of Jesus' advocacy; the frequency of Jesus' advocacy; and the result of Jesus' advocacy. The points will be discussed in that order before a conclusive application and a related prayer are made.

1. The Nature of Jesus' Advocacy

God is the Judge: "For the LORD is our judge, the LORD is our lawgiver, the LORD is our king; it is he who will save us."[143] There are four characteristics that every judge must posses: Objective-open-mindedness (not being biased); fairness; independence (an impartial judge);[144] and decisiveness. However, any judge who also adds righteousness to these qualities, is a rare gift in any justice system. God is said to be a righteous judge: "God is a righteous judge, a God who displays his wrath every day."[145] This means that God cannot be bribed, and neither does He fall for human intrigues and innuendos.

The quality of righteousness in judgeship, also means that wrong will be punished and good will be rewarded. We know that God does not side with evil, and anyone who considers what is evil to be good is said to be cursed: "Woe to

---

[143] Isaiah 33:22
[144] See 1 Peter 1:17
[145] Psalm 7:11

those who call evil good and good evil, who put darkness for light and light for darkness, who put bitter for sweet and sweet for bitter."[146] And God does not change in regard to this: ""I the LORD do not change."[147] This, essentially, means that when we sin, we must be punished. For there are only two possibilities – it is either we change and behave good to avert God's wrath and punishment, or God changes and overlooks our evil.

Since, as established, God does not change, it remained that we changed and did good to be saved. However, we were incapable of doing good. God, to save humanity, did not change but He transformed Himself into a man.[148] As a substitute man, He incurred God's wrath on the Cross to save humanity: "He himself bore our sins in his body on the tree, that we might die to sin and live to righteousness. By his wounds you have been healed."[149] The salvation, thus, secured, is total: "For Christ also suffered once for sins, the righteous for the unrighteous, that he might bring us to God, being put to death in the flesh but made alive in the spirit."[150] But it requires positive acceptance for this gift to be effective. Those who reject God's offer of

---

[146] Isaiah 5:20
[147] Malachi 3:6
[148] See John 1:14 and Philippians 2:8 ff
[149] 1 Peter 2:24; also see Hebrews 12:2 or Romans 5:8
[150] 1 Peter 3:18

salvation will still incur God's wrath.[151] Those who accept God's free gift of salvation – or Jesus Christ – remain righteous before God because of the advocacy work of Jesus Christ through the Holy Spirit who actions the process of sanctification.

With regards to sin, God's wrath still burns. This quality makes God fearful: "Who is like unto thee, O LORD, among the gods? who is like thee, glorious in holiness, fearful in praises, doing wonders?"[152] And again, "Let all the earth fear the Lord; let all the inhabitants of the world stand in awe of him!"[153] However, the fear of God is also the basis of His mercy: "And his mercy is for those who fear him from generation to generation."[154] In other words, those who fear, a *fearful* God, can also access His mercy. This balance is what has preserved God's just rule for millennia. Like God, a good judge should have both wrath and love. Mercy has no value without wrath. Possessing only one without the other, makes justice a mockery.

The balance between wrath and love is called righteousness. God's throne is founded on righteousness: "Righteousness and justice are the foundation of thy throne."[155] This

---

[151] See John 3:16
[152] Exodus 15:11
[153] Psalm 33:8
[154] Luke 1:50
[155] Psalms 89:14

wrath/love combination of God's throne, makes advocacy there a challenge for weak, immoral, and frail humanity. Only Jesus Christ possesses the requisite character and quality to advocate before the throne of God.

The thing that separated humanity from God was sin. Christ lived His entire earthly life without sin, yet God made Him sin: "For he hath made him to be sin for us, who knew no sin; that we might be made the righteousness of God in him."[156] That simply means that Christ bore all our sins and that sin was dealt with once and for all. And yet, there was no sin found in Jesus: "And ye know that he was manifested to take away our sins; and in him is no sin."[157] There is just no sin in Him, but He never sinned as well: "Who did not sin, neither was guile found in his mouth."[158] He did not just sin, not because He had no opportunity to sin, He was tempted like us but He overcame all temptations: "For we have not an high priest which cannot be touched with the feeling of our infirmities; but was in all points tempted like as we are, yet without sin."[159]

Thus, only Jesus is qualified to appear before a righteous God on our behalf. There is no accusation brought by Satan (accuser of the

---

[156] 2 Corinthians 5:21
[157] 1 John 3:5
[158] 1 Peter 2:22
[159] Hebrews 4:15

brethren)[160] that can tilt the scale against man. And the reason is simple, "Therefore, there is now no condemnation for those who are in Christ Jesus."[161] The authority to represent those who are in Him, came from Jesus' redemption work on the Cross: "Who will bring any charge against God's elect? It is God who justifies. Who is there to condemn us? For Christ Jesus, who died, and more than that was raised to life, is at the right hand of God— and He is interceding for us."[162] Our lawyer in heaven is Jesus Christ, and the authority to represent us was duly earned through His suffering, death and, of course, resurrection. No insinuations, no innuendos, no frivolity, and no accusatory oratory of Satan can win against Christ's advocacy on our behalf.

2. The Frequency of Jesus' Advocacy

The power and joy of Jesus' advocacy rests on this verse: "Therefore he is able to save completely those who come to God through him, because he always lives to intercede for them."[163] The phrase, "lives to intercede for them," indicates ministry. Our Lord Jesus Christ's ministry or vocation is that of a lawyer. That is the job He currently occupies in heaven.

---

[160] Revelation 12:10
[161] Romans 8:1
[162] Romans 8: 33-34
[163] Hebrews 7:25

The denotation in the present tense means that He does this frequently, basically, always. The Bible also says that He is at God's right hand, "interceding for us."[164] This is denoted in the present-continuous tense – meaning that Jesus Christ undertakes this ministry continuously. He never takes a break; He never goes on vacation. He is always representing us.

3. The Result of Jesus' Advocacy

There are numerous benefits or results of Jesus Christ advocating on our behalf. Only five will be offered in this discourse. First, Satan's weapons against us fail: "'No weapon forged against you will prevail, and you will refute every tongue that accuses you. This is the heritage of the servants of the LORD, and this is their vindication from me,' declares the LORD."[165]

Second, after Christ took over this duty in heaven, no longer is Satan a convincing force against believers: "Then the angel showed me Joshua the high priest standing before the angel of the LORD, with Satan standing at his right hand to accuse him. And the LORD said to Satan: 'The LORD rebukes you, Satan! Indeed, the LORD, who has chosen Jerusalem, rebukes you! Is not this man a firebrand snatched from the fire?' Now Joshua was dressed in filthy

---

[164] Romans 8:34
[165] Isaiah 54:17; see also

garments as he stood before the angel."[166] Joshua did not have victory because he stood before God in his own filth. Not now, not anymore. Now, we stand before God through Christ. God sees Christ when we go before Him. Paul prayed, "For this reason I bow my knees before the Father, from whom every family in heaven and on earth derives its name."[167] Paul calls the people of God, a "family." We are adopted into the family of God. We have now intrinsic authority.

Third, we now appear before God within the authority of Jesus Christ and of our membership in God's family: "I have given you authority to trample on snakes and scorpions and to overcome all the power of the enemy; nothing will harm you."[168] We are no longer outsiders; we belong to the family of God, as such, we have privileges, rights, and authority.

Fourth, Jesus Christ accepts to represent us free of charge and at all times: "All those the Father gives me will come to me, and whoever comes to me I will never drive away."[169] In our earthly affairs, sometimes lawyers are too expensive to represent our interests. Not with Christ, His services are free, and He is available to everyone who needs such legal or advocacy work. He

---

[166] Zechariah 3:2
[167] Ephesians 3:14-15
[168] Luke 10:19
[169] John 6:37

invites, "Come to me, all you who are weary and burdened, and I will give you rest."[170] And He assures, "And I will do whatever you ask in my name, so that the Father may be glorified in the Son."[171]

And fifth, Jesus Christ's lawyering sets those He represents free: "So if the Son sets you free, you will be free indeed."[172] In other words, Jesus Christ wins all the time. Those He sets free must know they are free, then they will be free, indeed: "Then you will know the truth, and the truth will set you free."[173] This freedom defeats Satan and death: "For in Christ Jesus the law of the Spirit of life set you free from the law of sin and death."[174] We are no longer slaves of any man or Satan; we have become slaves of Christ and of righteousness: "For he who was a slave when he was called by the Lord is the Lord's freedman. Conversely, he who was a free man when he was called is Christ's slave."[175] Know this freedom, and stand firm, established in it: "It is for freedom that Christ has set us free. Stand firm, then, and do not be encumbered once more by a yoke of slavery."[176] How

---

[170] Matthew 11:28
[171] John 14:13
[172] John 8:36
[173] John 8:32
[174] Romans 8:2
[175] 1 Corinthians 7:22
[176] Galatians 5:1

amazing this victory, freedom and advocacy. To Jesus be all the glory.

Conclusion & Application

The new ministry Jesus Christ undertakes on our behalf includes lawyering for us. He represents our spiritual interests before the judgment seat of God. In Christ, we have had mercy, and, therefore, we are triumphant in both death and judgment. And this is literally, we will not be harmed by the Judgment Day – we have passed from death to life. All this is through Christ, our great advocate. This intercessory ministry of Jesus Christ also preserves the accruement of His works of redemption. Christ is a good investor – He does not abandon His investments to chance. He protects His investments and secures their good fortune and profit. He lives for us, and if we sin, we have a ready and available advocate. This way, sin is purged continually. Our role is an easy one – to report to Him so He can open a docket with the Father. All we have to do is confess and ask for forgiveness each time we sin. Child of God, do not become tired of asking for forgiveness, because He does not become tired of advocating for you. This, too, is a manifestation of His Grace – even where sin abounds, His Grace just goes further. Jesus, has single-handedly transformed God's judgment seat into a throne of mercy. Yes, in Christ alone and to Him be all the glory, Amen!

Related Prayer

Dear Heavenly Father,

We have many times wondered away from
your grace;
We have surely transgressed the beauty of
Your place;
Yet, despite all, You have not left us without
an advocate;
Oh, LORD, Jesus, and Jesus Christ alone, is
adequate.

In the name of Jesus, our Lord,
Amen.

ABOUT THE AUTHOR

Charles Mwewa (LLB, BA. Edu. + Engl., BA. Legal Studies, Cert. Law, DIBM., LLM.) is a Dad, author, and poet. Mwewa is the author of over 50 books and counting in all genres – fiction (novels), non-fiction and poetry. Mwewa, his wife, and their three girls, reside in the Capital City of Ottawa, Canada

Websites:
charlesmwewa.com
acpress.ca

Facebook:
https://www.facebook.com/authorcharlesmwewa

Email:
info@acpress.ca

Amazon
https://www.amazon.ca/dp/1988251303

INDEX